MY THOUGHTS

AND

MEMORIES

PUBLISHING COMPANY

ISBN: 978-0-6151-7480-8

Edited and Published by: Walter Burchett, BA

www.Crossover-Ministries-Publishing.com

TABLE OF CONTENTS

POEMS

ABOUT THE AUTHOR

My name is Isabel Mateus, I was born in 1972 in a small village in Portugal. My parents didn't have that much, but were still happy with what they had. They had love for each other which conquers all. Both mom and dad were very hard workers. When I was just turning one year old we arrived in Canada. It wasn't that easy to live in a new country. We arrived here on October 23, 1973. Right after that my mom started working. My dad fell ill in the first five months, it wasn't that great of a start, but then soon after dad was better, he started back to work. We were raised Catholic, but that all changed one day in 1980, mom became a Christian. I went to school here, and started writing in high school during my drama class. I have been inspired ever since, in between life experiences, I have created these poems to share my journey.

I am a single mom of a great seven year old little boy that I love so very much! Without my son I don't know where I would be. It has been a very long journey in such a short time, many joys and many tears, but through it all I never lost faith. I know in my heart I can make it, and so can you. I believe these writings will encourage you through all things and maybe even put a smile on your face in those roller coaster times. I want to express my sincere thanks to all my family and friends for their unconditional support and love. I hope to make a difference in other peoples lives and tell them they can make it as long as you believe and put God first in everything you do. This is for all of you, enjoy reading, "*My Thoughts And Memories!*"

INTRODUCTION

The introduction of these poems are what I have been though in my life and many thing along the way. I hope these poems can do some good to the ones reading them, sharing my life with you as well.

A MAN OF GOD: I wrote about my spiritual father that is my pastor. He as help me with so much in my life, he is a very good friend to me and I am like a daughter to him.

BEFORE YOU WERE BORN: A poem I wrote when I was carrying my son, and how motherhood came to me.

DOCTOR SAID: About me with a learning disability I was born with and the doctor told my parents that I would never make it to high school, but I proved the doctor wrong.

FATHER: To amortize all fathers, I did this for my dad.

FRIENDS: About the friend I had in school and the friendships that I left behind.

FIRST TIME GOING OUT: Talks about when I started dating boys. I found out the hard way that boys don't have just one girlfriend they have more then one.

GETTING TO KNOW YOU: Love and trust, finding someone that cares for you.

HAVE I TOLD YOU LATELY: Caring about other's feelings.

GOD: So wonderful I cannot express it, talks about every day life.

I CHERISH: About how much things mean to me in my life.

I HAVE A FRIEND CALLED: When I was sitting on my bed just thinking about my life and where it is going now. You always have a friend that understands you if your friends on Earth can't.

I MET SOMEONE NEW: I was in high school at the time, dating this wonderful person.

I'M STANDING HERE ALONE: How my son's father left me alone raising our son.

IT WASN'T MY FAULT: About my dad, the problem that he had with drinking.

JUST EIGHTEEN: How I lost someone very close to me. My own cousin died in a car crash.

LOVE: How people are just honest in what they do.
MEETING YOU FOR THE FIRST TIME: Dating and all.
MISSING YOU: To people that miss each other.
MOM'S: About the mother love.
YOU SAID: About breaking up.
MY BELOVED: A few words out of the bible.
MY GRANDFATHER: About my grandfather.
ON THIS VERY SPECIAL DAY: About love.
ROSES ARE RED: Falling in love again, don't loose hope of falling in love.
HERE I AM: Being humble to God.
THINKING BACK: I was going out with my first love and the memories I left behind.
TWO HEARTS: When I found what I was looking for.
UNTIL THE END OF TIME: About love and trust.
WHEN I FALL IN LOVE: Special because it brings back good memories.
WHEN I LOOK IN YOUR EYES: The first poem I did when I was with my son's father.
WHEN I TAKE: Talks about love.
YOUR EYES: Talks about what you really want to hear.
AMAZING GRACE: Is a poem that talks about how accepted the lord at the age of 12 years old.
BLUE EYES BOY: It talks about my son who has blue eyes
I HAD A DREAM: It talks about a dream I had that left me thinking about.
JUST US TWO: Is about my son and me just us two and how I love him so much.
WHAT IS LIFE: This poem teaches us about life and how we got through life.
I STAND HERE ALONE: Is how my son's father left me alone.

MY THOUGHTS

AND

MEMORIES

A MAN OF GOD

A Man of God,
Is what you are.
You are always,
Praying for us.
You give us guidance,
All along the way.

You encourage us,
To do our best.
In everything,
We do.
And if,
We go out of line.

You tell us,
"Be careful."
In what we do,
I thank God.
That we have you,
In our lives.

And we all love you,
Just the same way.
You love us,
A man of God.
That's,
What you are.

You listen,

To God.
And He speaks,
To your heart.
To say,
God loves us so.

You are a wonderful person,
And a good friend.
To us all,
May God keep you.
On His path,
And give you strength.

To carry on,
The way you are.
Doing God's work,
And He will give you.
All the blessing,
That you need in your life.

BEFORE YOU WERE BORN

Hello,
My little one.
You don't know me yet,
But, in time you will.
I am,
Your mother.

The one,

Who is carrying you.
You are a blessing,
To me.
Even though,
You are not here yet.

And you,
Are growing.
Inside of me,
Everyday.
I wonder,
Who you are.

And what,
You will look like.
And,
As I talk to you.
I know,
That you hear me.

My little one,
Inside of me.
I love you so,
And I can't wait.
To give birth,
To you.

As the months,
Go by.
And you're growing,
Inside.

I pray,
That you are a boy.

That's what's,
In my heart.
Feels like you,
Are my little one.
Now that time,
Has come.

To give birth,
To you.
My little one,
The hours.
Are so long now,
And the pain.

Is unbearable,
But I know.
That without pain,
There wouldn't be you.
So the hour,
Is near.

And here you come,
Out of me.
I carry all the joy that you are here,
And I see you for the first time.
In my arms,
A little baby.

That you are,
So sweet,
And handsome.
To his mother,
And what a blessing.

As well as that of,
A mother's love.
The pain that,
She goes through.
To give birth,
To a son.

The son,
That she.
Loves the most,
Before you.
Were even,
Born.

DOCTOR SAID

I was,
Five years old.
When the doctor,
Told my parents.
I couldn't go,
To high school.

I had a,
Learning disability.
When I was in,

Elementary school.
I used to,
Do things like.

I have,
My hairdressing diploma.
I am proud,
Of myself!
I have accomplished,
My goals.

Whatever the doctor,
Told my parents.
My parents,
Wouldn't accept it.
I proved,
The doctor wrong.

Never,
Ever.
Believe everything,
You hear.
Especially,
With a doctor!

FATHERS

Fathers,
Are everything.
You want,
In a man.

They're there,
When you.
Need them,
And when you.

Need a hug,
Fathers.
Talk to you,
They understand.

What you are,
Going through.
Most of all,
They love you.

FRIENDS

Friends are true,
They are helpful.
You can,
Depend on them.

Sometimes,

You have good times.
Friends are close,
They are caring.

Friends are loveable,
Old friends are special.
New friends are nice,
Friends understand.

They go through,
Good and bad times.
Friends are logout,
They are caring.

Friends are kind,
Friends are always there.
When you need them,
Friends make you happy.

You have parties,
With them.
They accept you,
With problems.

Friends,
Are everything.
You want,
In one.

FIRST TIME GOING OUT

It was,
The first time.
I was going out,
With a guy.

I was so scared,
But guys don't bite.
I thought they did,
But it wasn't that bad.

He said sweet things to me,
Like you look pretty.
We went to the movies,
But after two weeks.

He didn't want,
To go out.
With me,
Anymore.

I didn't understand why then,
I still don't now.
Oh well,
It was his loss.

GETTING TO KNOW YOU

Getting to know you now,

And you say.
That you love me,
It is true.

Getting to know you,
And it makes.
Me feel happy,
That I have you.

Getting to know you,
Makes me feel.
Like you mean,
The world to me.

Getting to know you,
Better each time.
I see you,
You know that is true.

Well,
I have one thing to say.
I am happy,
That I met someone like you.

HAVE I TOLD YOU LATELY

Have I told you lately,
That I love you.
Have I told you lately,
That I really do care.

Have I told you lately,
That you mean.
So much,
To me.

Have I told you lately,
That I still care.
Have I told you lately,
That you're the only one for me.

Yes,
You are the one.
I love,
Have I told you?

GOD

God made the earth,
God made the trees.
God made the birds,
And God made the bees.

God made the seas,
God made you and me.
And everything,
We see.

I CHERISH

I cherish,
What I have.
I cherish,
What I can give.

To you,
I cherish.
Your love,
That is so true.

I cherish,
Your song.
That you gave,
To me.

I cherish,
Your sweet melody.
That you sang,
To me.

I cherish,
Everything above.
The most important thing I cherish is you,
You are always there when I need you.

A shoulder to cry on,
I cherish the bond.
That we have that is so strong,

And sometimes it is so hard to let go.
Most of all I will cherish you,
Until the end of my life.

I HAVE A FRIEND CALLED

I have a friend and my friend is always there for me,
He listens to what I say.
He sees what I do,
And He is always there.

You don't see Him, but He is there,
When you are going through rough times.
He doesn't leave you,
He is always there to help you and guide you along the way.

My friend is a good friend,
He loves you very much.
Sometimes we forget that He's there,
He doesn't forget about us.

He 's a special friend of mine,
And His name is above all names.
He is called Jesus,
And He can be your friend too.

I MET SOMEONE NEW

I met someone new, boy,
It was you.

You came into my life when I was feeling down,
I'd say that was true.

I love you boy,
I love you to the max.
We were bound to be together,
That day that I met you.

You looked so well boy,
And so fine too.
It was like a dream come true,
Now we are together boy.

At last, that dream did come true,
For me and you.
We talked on the phone almost four hours,
I didn't want to leave, I didn't want to say good-bye to you.

But I know better than that,
So we say.
Good–bye,
And see you later.

I'M STANDING HERE ALONE

I'm standing here alone in my world so cold,
And no one to talk to.
I sit here and think,
Lots of things that happened in my life.

Still without you I go on,
How could you hurt me like this.
And say that you care about me,
You said that you wouldn't let me go.

And I believed you so,
How stupid was I to believe so many lies.
That you told me, now still alone,
I go on and raising our son alone, I go on.

The gift that you gave me is too precious and so sweet,
The little boy that I call my son loves me as I am.
He doesn't even say your name,
Even though you are not here with us.

That little boy has someone,
That loves him dearly.
And that person is me, his mom,
Just us is how it's going to be.

IT WASN'T MY FAULT

When I was growing up my dad had a problem,

His problem was drinking, he was an alcoholic.
He used to swear and abuse my mother,
But not in front of me.

I hated when they argued,
I would go to my room and cry.
I thought it was my fault,
That my dad was drinking.

I blamed myself,
What was I supposed to think.
I was only seven years old,
When this happened.

Now he doesn't drink,
He paid the price for his drinking.
He has diabetes,
Kidney and liver damage.

He's overweight, and has water inside the knee,
Sometimes, because of these problems, he can't go to work.
I'm glad that he doesn't drink anymore,
Now that I'm older, I realize it wasn't my fault father drank.

JUST EIGHTEEN

Just eighteen,
And very young.
When the car,
Hit him.

Just eighteen,
When it happened.
He died,
He was just starting his life.

It stopped,
He never got.
To see it,
Just eighteen.

When it happened,
This way.
I never got,
To say goodbye.

LOVE

Love is like the sea,
It is the only way to be.
Everyday when you are with me,
Even to this very day.

We are loving people,
Open and honest.
Very kind and easygoing,
...And understanding.

MEETING YOU FOR THE FIRST TIME

Meeting you,
For the first time.
In my life,
I hardly know you.

But we talked,
On the telephone.
For hours,
And.

I still wonder,
How you are.
On the other side,
I wonder.

If you feel,
The same way.
About me,
The only thing I know is your name.

You probably felt,
The same way.
When you,
Saw me to.

You probably thought.
'Who is that girl?

Looking fine,
Too!'

Boy,
You and me.
We both,
Made history that day.

And now,
We are together.
Forever,
To the end, boy.

MISSING YOU

I am,
Missing you.
Yes,
It's true.

The way,
You make me feel.
When I am,
With you.

You make me,
Feel safe.
That 's true,
I am with you.

And you mean,
The world,
To me.
It's true.

I love you,
So much.
I love you,
So baby.

Don't let me go,
Out of your life, Ok?
I will always love you,
Until the end of time.

MOM'S

Mom's,
Are always there.
When you need them,
They are helpful.

When you,
Are sad.
They're,
Always there for you.

Sometimes,
Mom's.
Are there,

When you need a hand.

They,
Are there.
When you do,
Something wrong.

But,
Most of all.
They love you,
Always.

YOU SAID

You said,
That you loved me.
From the start,
And you said.

We'd never be apart,
You said.
We will always,
Be together.

But now we're apart,
Until this day.
I don't know,
Why we're apart.

MY BELOVED

My beloved,
Loves me.
And I love,
My beloved.

My beloved,
Hears.
What I have,
To say.

My beloved's voice,
Is like the wind.
Blowing,
As gentle as can be.

My beloved,
Is the shepherd.
Of His sheep,
And my beloved.

Takes great care,
And joy.
In them,
Holy is my beloved's kingdom.

As beautiful,
As silver and gold.
Blessed,
Is my beloved.

My beloved's mercy,
Never ends.

My beloved,
Is like.
The morning,
Sun.

That shines,
All day long.
My heart,
Is my beloved's.

And,
My beloved's.
Heart,
Is mine.

If you are wondering,
Who I'm talking about.
It my Savoir,
Jesus Christ is our Lord.

MY GRANDFATHER
(In Loving Memory Of My Grandfather)

My grandfather is a very kind man,
He plays with his granddaughters all the time.
His smile, Oh, his smile,
I can't forget.

Well too bad he's gone,
Where did he go? I don't know.
Maybe to Heaven or maybe to Hell,
I don't know, I miss him though.

I wish he was still here, but he's not,
I remember the good times, Oh, those good times we had.
I will love him even though he's gone,
He is still in my heart.

ON THIS VERY SPECIAL DAY

On this very special day,
That is called, Valentine's Day.
Boy, just want to say,
That I love you so.

And, I can't let you go,
Boy, will you stay with me?
You and me, you will see,
That all I want is to be your girl.

Let it be so,
On this very special day.
That is the best day of your life,
Is having me by your side.

Let me be the one today,
I love you on this special day.
Happy Valentine's Day,
From me to you.

So,
My valentine, tThe answer is 'Yes!'
I will love you forever, Baby,
I,
Love you so!

ROSES ARE RED

Roses are red, violets are blue,
Sugar is sweet, and so are you.
Roses are red, violets are blue,
I am so lucky, to have a wonderful man as you.

Roses are red, violets are blue,
No one is as wonderful and special as you!
Roses are red, violets are blue.
When I meet this special someone who made me feel,
So wonderful and good inside, and full.

Roses are red, violets are blue,

I am falling in love.
And feeling high as a dove,
As I hear his voice, he is my one and only choice.

HERE I AM

Here I am waiting for you,
Here I am humble and true.
Here I am still loving you,
Here I am carrying for you.

Here I am taking care of you,
Here I am your child so true.
Here I am willing to help you,
Here I am the one that died for your sins.

Here I am I will take care of you,
Here I am.
Your God,
So true.

THINKING BACK

Thinking back when we were going out,
You said that we would be together.
Thinking back when you bought me something,
And you said that you loved me.

I was a fool to believe that you loved me,
You were playing around with me.

You didn't love me, you probably loved someone else,

But now you're gone,
And I can go on.
Living,
Without you.

TWO HEARTS

Two hearts that beats as one,
Two hearts that belong together.
Two hearts are meant for each other,
Two hearts love one another.

Two hearts that mean so much,
Two hearts will never part.
Two hearts will always be,
Two hearts is the only way to be.
Two hearts until the end.

UNTIL THE END OF TIME

I'll be there for you,
And baby it's so true.
So I will love you,
Until the end of time.

So take my hand and you will see,
That my love is so true.
And baby you will see,
I am the one for you.

Because I will be by your side forever, and ever,
Because you make me feel like I am the one for you.
I will make you understand I am the one,
You want to be with baby.

I am here for you, so be the one, for me baby,
Don't you let me go?
Because I love you so,
I can't live without you.

So baby say you will stay with me,
And I will be the happiest girl in the world.
So I will stay with you until the end of time,
Baby, it's so true and I will always love you,
Until the end of time, yes it's true.

WHEN I FALL IN LOVE

When I fall in love it will be forever,
Yes, it will be with you.
You are my life, you are my joy,
You are what a girl would look for in a boy.

You shine like the sun on a warm summer day,
You take care of me when I feel sad.

You make me feel like a winner,
And not a loser.

Because you stand by me,
Always support me when I am down.
You say that you love me,
I know that's true because I feel the same way.
A few words to you too,
I love you to the max, Baby face, I always will.

WHEN I LOOK IN YOUR EYES

When I look your eyes,
When I see you smile.
Your tender touch of your kiss,
Makes me feel so happy inside.

As you say that you love me with all your heart,
My love my love, so, we meet for the first time.
I'm so happy that you are going to be mine,
And that we are going to be together.

At last, forever and ever, we will be together.
This is my vow to you my love.
Together at last to the end of our old age,
Then God will send us to Him.

WHEN I TALK

When I talk,
To you.
On the phone,
Something.

Wonderful,
Happens.
To me,
When we talk.

You make me feel,
So happy.
And,
So funny inside.

Like,
It was.
The first time,
I talked to you.

But it isn't,
You always make.
My rainy days,
Shine.

And when,
I need a friend.
To talk too,

Oh baby!

I know,
That you.
Will be there,
For me.

When I,
Need you.
You know,
That I'll do.

The same,
For you.
I will be there,
For you too.

YOUR EYES

Your eyes,
Sparkle.
In the,
Moonlight.

Your eyes say,
So much more.
They say,
'I care'.

'Sadness eyes',

Say.
What you want,
Them to say.

But,
One thing.
They don't say,
Is what.

I want,
To hear.
From you?
What?

I want to hear,
Through your eyes.
'I love you,
Forever'.

AMAZING GRACE

Amazing Grace,
How sweet.
The sound,
That saved someone just like me.

I was at church one Sunday Service,
One morning in 1985.
I was 12 at the time,
And it was a normal service.

Or I thought it was,
But I felt very happy.
And I didn't know why,
Or what was going on within me.

That Sunday Morning in 1985,
but one thing was for sure.
I had never had,
Such a wonderful feeling in my life.

That day I went,
To the front.
And I accepted God,
As my Savior.

The song,
'Amazing Grace' says.
'Once I was lost',
But now that I have accepted God into my life.

I am found,
Yes.
I am found,
and God.

Is still,
To this day.
In my life,
I was baptized in 1991 as well.

So I have a wonderful feeling,

To do that in my life.
And never, never look back,
God loves me.

And no matter what,
Your problem is.
He is always there,
For you as well.

Just ask Him,
And He will give you.
All the blessing,
That you need.

Yes,
I am found.
And God loves me for me,
He loves you too.

Just believe,
In yourself and you will see.
That God is the only,
Way to be.

BLUE EYES BOY

Blue eyes boy,
Came into my world.
So innocent and pure,
Blue eyes boy so little and new.

Blue eyes boy,
So handsome.
And special,
To me.

You'll always be,
My blue eyes boy.
For all eternity,
Blue eyes boy.
Growing,
To be a child.

My blue eyes boy,
And having his mama's love.
Blue eyes boy,
I hope you'll never grow up.

And stay as a child,
Your my blue eyes boy.
Humble,
And all mine.

My son,
My blue eyes boy.
Be who you are,
And never change who you are.

Be the best,
That you can be.
You're my,
Blue eyes boy.

The one,
That mama loves.
And adores,
Her blue eyes boy.

And that's the truth,
My blue eyes boy.
You're,
My son.

So true,
Your the best thing.
That happened to me,
You're my blue eyes boy.

So wonderful and true,
My blue eyes boy.
Mama will always love you,
My blue eyes boy.

I HAD A DREAM

I had a dream,
In my dream.
I was in a garden,
It was a beautiful garden.

With trees,
Flower's.

And animals,
Of different kinds.

I was feeding the animals,
In this garden.
And there was a table,
There as well.

As I was feeling the animals,
I heard a voice that told me.
Can you give me some water,
To drink?

I turned around,
To see a man.
But I didn't see,
his face.

I gave him the water,
And then I went back to work.
I looked back,
To see if the man was there.

But he wasn't,
All of a sudden.
I saw a creature,
So ugly that I just stood there.

This creature,
Had a face of a crocodile.
And a body of a snake,

If I told you that.

You'd think I was crazy,
But I did dream of this.
And the creature,
Wanted to get me.

But he couldn't get to me,
He tried to.
But he couldn't,
I believe the man was Jesus himself.

And that was when I woke up,
I was still in my bed.
I don't know if that was a dream,
or a vision that I had.

And I will never know,
But the only one.
That knows,
Is GOD Himself.

JUST US TWO

Just us two here, just us two,
For the past six years now.
And it has been some very hard times as well,
As some very good times.

Just us two, a mom and her loving little boy,
That she loves with all her heart and soul.

She will do almost anything,
For her son.

That she loves very much,
She gave birth to him.
She's seen how he is,
Growing up to be a very young man.

But he is still a little boy,
Of seven years old.
But even though,
He is that old.

She sees his future,
Being whatever he wants to be.
He always says,
That he likes to be a police officer.

Or a bus driver,
Or a soccer player.
But whatever he becomes,
I know I will always be proud of him.

He is my little one,
Know that he is.
And I know that he will be,
A very kind and loving son.

To his mom,
Just the two of us.
We love each other,

Very much.

Just us two,
Mother.
And son,
And one day.

He will become,
A parent as well.
And then,
Will he understand,
What being a parent is all about?

Just us two,
A mother and her son.
Yes, just us two,
Just for now.

WHAT IS LIFE

What is life, what is it all about,
What is it, and what does it mean?
Life is a circle, life is the most precious thing you can have,
You live, you grow, and you die from it.

Life is all that and so much more,
You learn from life.
You teach other about life,
And life can heal you as well.

Life is so pure and life is so good,

Life is the most wonderful thing you can have.
Life is the most beautiful thing you can have,
You have to cherish life itself.

Or you don't know how it will turn out at the end,
So just cherish it as much as you can.
And you will see,
Where life will lead you.

I STAND HERE ALONE

I stand here alone in my world so cold,
And no one to talk to I sit here and think of a lot of things.
That happened in my life and still without you I go on,
How could you hurt me like this and say that you care.

When you said that you wouldn't let me go,
And I believed you so how stupid I was to believe.
So many lies that you told me, now I'm still alone,
I go on raising our son alone, I go on.

The gift that you gave me is too precise,
And so sweet, the little boy that I call my son.
Loves me as I am, and he doesn't even say your name,
Even though you are not here with us.

That little boy has someone that loves him dearly,
And that person is me, his mom.
Just that and us,
Is how it's going to be.

www.ingramcontent.com/pod-product-compliance
Lightning Source LLC
Chambersburg PA
CBHW031335040426
42443CB00005B/349